IT'S ELECTRIC!

Making a Circuit

Chris Oxlade

Raintree

www.raintreepublishers.co.uk
Visit our website to find out
more information about
Raintree books.

To order:
☎ Phone 0845 6044371
🖹 Fax +44 (0) 1865 312263
🖥 Email myorders@raintreepublishers.co.uk

Customers from outside the UK please telephone +44 1865 312262

Raintree is an imprint of Capstone Global Library Limited,
a company incorporated in England and Wales having its
registered office at 7 Pilgrim Street, London, EC4V 6LB
– Registered company number: 6695582

Text © Capstone Global Library Limited 2012
First published in hardback in 2012
First published in paperback in 2013
The moral rights of the proprietor have been asserted.

Edited by Daniel Nunn, Rebecca Rissman, and Catherine Veitch
Designed by Joanna Hinton-Malivoire
Picture research by Elizabeth Alexander
Production by Eirian Griffiths
Originated by Capstone Global Library Ltd
Printed and bound in China by Leo Paper Products Ltd

ISBN 978 1 406 23228 8 (hardback)
15 14 13 12
10 9 8 7 6 5 4 3 2

ISBN 978 1 406 23233 2 (paperback)
16 15 14 13 12
10 9 8 7 6 5 4 3 2 1

British Library Cataloguing in Publication Data

Oxlade, Chris.
Making a circuit. -- (It's electric!)
621.3'192-dc22
A full catalogue record for this book is available from the
British Library.

Acknowledgements

The author and publisher are grateful to the following for
permission to reproduce photographs: Alamy p. 29 (© Pixel
Youth Movement 4); © Capstone Publishers pp. 4 (Karon
Dubke), 5 (Karon Dubke), 8 (Karon Dubke), 9 (Karon Dubke),
10 (Karon Dubke), 11 (Karon Dubke), 12 (Karon Dubke),
14 (Karon Dubke), 16 (Karon Dubke), 21 (Karon Dubke),
23 (Karon Dubke), 25 (Karon Dubke); iStockphoto pp. 13
(© Jivko Kazakov), 17 (© bojan fatur); Photolibrary p, 27
(Stockbroker); Shutterstock pp. 6 (© sergioconsoli), 15 (© Shi
Yali), 26 (© Adrian Britton), 28 (© Naturaldigital).

Cover photograph of pupils and a teacher in class
with an electronic project reproduced with permission
of Shutterstock (© Monkey Business Images). Design
background feature reproduced with permission of
Shutterstock (© echo3005).

The publisher would like to thank Terence Alexander for his
assistance in the preparation of this book.

Every effort has been made to contact copyright holders
of material reproduced in this book. Any omissions will
be rectified in subsequent printings if notice is given to
the publisher.

Disclaimer

Contents

Some words are shown in bold, **like this**.
You can find them in the glossary on page 30.

Electricity and circuits

Electricity is one of our most useful **resources**. It powers all sorts of machines, from pocket torches to express trains. It also lights up our homes and streets.

Electricity powers the complicated circuits in this mobile phone.

When you touch the wire in this game, you make a loop that electricity can flow around. This makes a **buzzer** sound.

Electricity flows through things to make them work. But it can only flow around a loop that is complete. The loop is called an electric **circuit**.

Conductors and insulators

Electricity flows through the copper in the middle of these cables.

Electricity cannot flow everywhere. It can flow through some materials, but not through others. Materials that electricity can flow through are called **conductors**. Most conductors are metals.

Electricity cannot flow through most materials. These materials are called **insulators**. The plastic on the outside of a cable is an insulator. It stops electricity from escaping.

Here are some common conductors and insulators:

Conductors	Insulators
copper	plastic
iron	ceramic
steel	glass
aluminium	wood
gold	paper
silver	rubber

A simple circuit

wire

battery

bulb

These are components used in a torch.

An electric **circuit** is made up of parts called **components**. The components are connected by wires. The electricity flows along the wires and through the components.

When components are connected together to make a circuit, electricity flows around the circuit. If there is a break in the circuit, the electricity stops flowing.

Electricity flows out of the **battery**, through the bulb and back to the battery.

Making electricity flow

Electricity doesn't just flow round **circuits** by itself. It needs a push to make it flow. In many things, such as torches and toys, the push comes from **batteries**.

Batteries push electricity around the circuits in this toy.

batteries

You can think of a battery as being like a pump for electricity. It's a bit like a water pump pushing water through a loop of a hose. The water goes around the hose and back to the pump.

The battery pushes electricity through the bulb.

Components

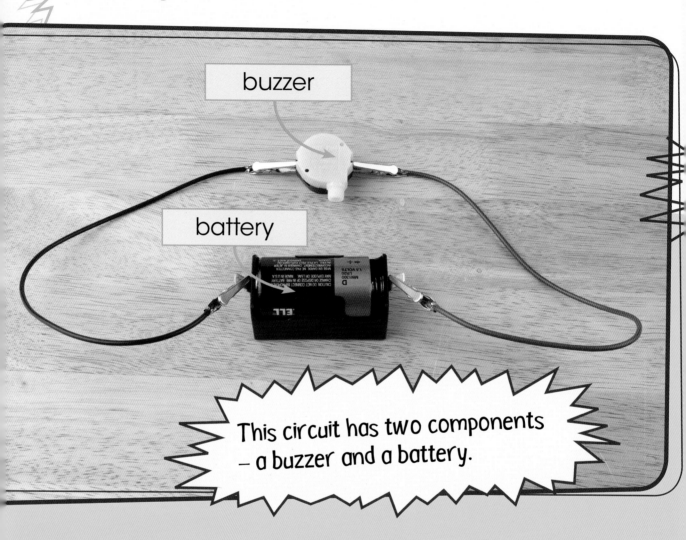

buzzer

battery

This circuit has two components – a buzzer and a battery.

Each **component** in an electric **circuit** does a job. **Batteries** and light bulbs are simple components. **Buzzers** and motors are components, too.

The circuits in machines such as televisions, radios, and computers are made up of hundreds of components. Many of the components are **microchips**.

microchip

Making connections

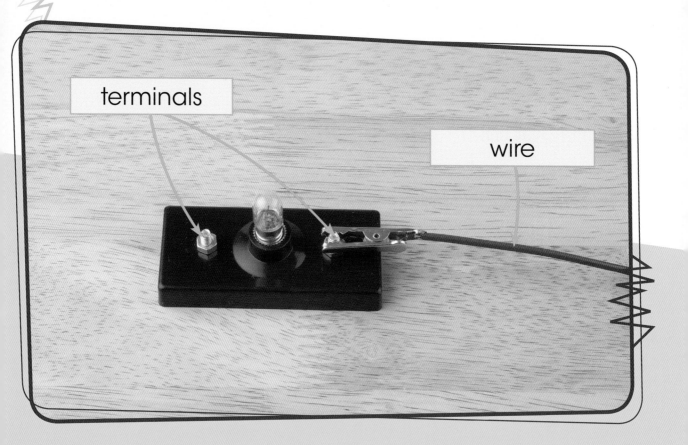

terminals

wire

The **components** in electric **circuits** need to be connected, or joined, so that electricity can flow between them. The connections between components such as **batteries** and bulbs are made with wire.

In complicated circuits, the connections are made with strips of metal on a plastic board. Most simple components have two places where wires or strips of metal connect them to a circuit. These are called **terminals**.

terminal

Switching on and off

The switch in this circuit turns the light bulb on and off.

switch

Electricity only flows around a **circuit** if the circuit is a complete loop. If there is a break in the loop, the **current** stops flowing. A switch is a **component** that lets us break a circuit when we want to.

Opening a switch breaks a circuit. This stops the electricity flowing. Closing a switch completes the circuit. This lets the electricity flow again.

There are many switches inside an aircraft cockpit.

Circuit diagrams

If you want to show somebody how to make an electric **circuit**, you can draw a picture of the circuit for them. This picture is called a **circuit diagram**. The **components** are shown by small pictures called symbols.

These are the symbols for some common components.

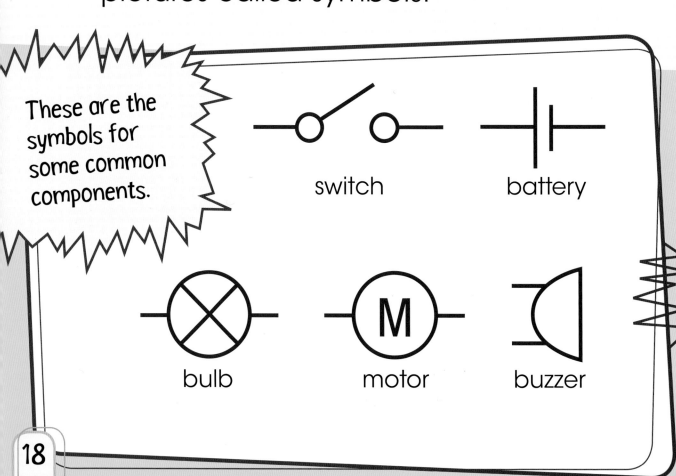

switch

battery

bulb

motor

buzzer

To draw a circuit diagram, you draw the symbols for the components in the circuit. Then you draw lines to show how the components are connected to each other.

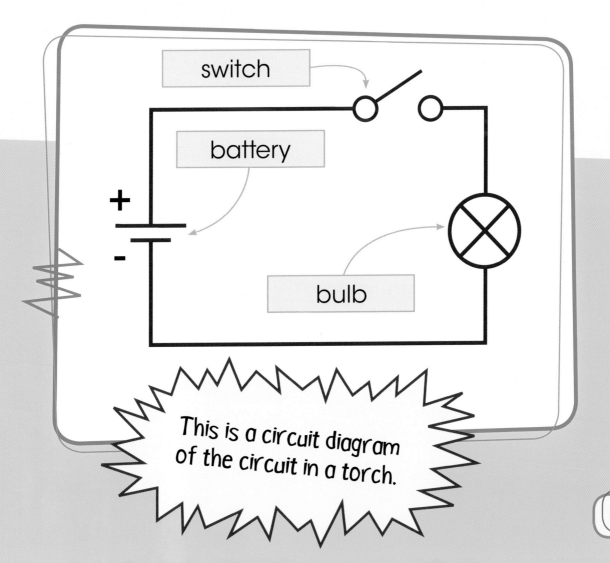

switch

battery

bulb

This is a circuit diagram of the circuit in a torch.

Building a circuit

Can you tell what components are in this circuit?

You can make a **circuit** by studying a **circuit diagram**. First you work out what **components** you need to make the circuit. You do this by looking at the symbols.

When you have found the components you need, you arrange them in the same way as they are in the diagram. The lines in the diagram show you how to connect the components together.

This circuit was made using the diagram on the opposite page.

Series and parallel

Series **circuits** and parallel circuits are two types of circuits. In a series circuit all the **components** are in one loop. The electricity flows through one component, then the next, until it gets back to where it started.

switch

battery

buzzers

In this series circuit the electricity flows through the **battery**, switch, and both **buzzers**.

The electricity flows through one bulb, then the other.

You can add a new component to a series circuit. Then all the electricity flowing in the circuit goes through the new component too. If you put two bulbs in series, they are only half as bright as one bulb.

In a parallel **circuit** the electricity splits up and goes different ways. Some of the electricity takes one path through the circuit. Some takes a different path through the circuit.

In this parallel circuit the electricity splits up and flows through both bulbs.

You can add a new **component** to a parallel circuit. Then some of the electricity flowing in the circuit flows through the new component, too. If you put two bulbs in parallel, the electricity splits up and flows through both bulbs.

Both bulbs light up.

Household circuits

This socket has a switch to turn the electricity on and off.

There are electric **circuits** in homes. The circuits are buried in the walls and floors. They carry electricity to wall sockets. When you plug an appliance, such as a toaster, into a socket, the appliance becomes part of the circuit.

There are circuits that carry electricity to the lights in your home. There are switches in the circuits. When you flick a light switch, a circuit is completed, and the light bulb comes on.

This electrician is putting electric circuits into a home.

Safety with circuits

The electricity that flows in household **circuits** is very powerful. If it goes through a person, it can badly injure them. It can even kill. Never push anything into an electricity socket or into a light fitting.

Danger
High voltage

⚠ 21308 KD

Warning signs show us that electricity is dangerous.

Most household circuits have a special safety feature. It's called a **circuit breaker**. If something goes wrong with the circuit or somebody gets an electric shock, the circuit breaker switches off the electricity.

Circuit breakers save lives by switching off electricity in an emergency.

Glossary

battery part that pushes electricity around a circuit

buzzer part that makes a buzzing sound when electricity flows through it

circuit loop that electricity flows around

circuit breaker safety part that switches off electricity if something goes wrong

circuit diagram diagram that shows how the parts in a circuit are connected

component something that does a job in an electric circuit, such as a battery or a bulb

conductor material that electricity can flow through

current flow of electricity through a wire or circuit

insulator material that electricity cannot flow through

microchip small part that contains a very complicated electric circuit

resource something that we use for making things and living our lives

Find out more

Books

Conductors and Insulators
(My World of Science), Angela Royston
(Raintree Publishers, 2008)

Electricity (Best Start in Science),
(Ticktock Books, 2009)

Electricity (Investigate), Chris Oxlade
(Raintree Publishers, 2008)

Websites

powerup.ukpowernetworks.co.uk/under-11.aspx
Interactive stuff on electricity from this UK company.

www.bbc.co.uk/schools/scienceclips/ages/6_7/electricity.shtml
Animated interactive games about electricity from the BBC.

www.switchedonkids.org.uk/
Lots of electricity activites, games, and puzzles.

Index